Greater Than a Tourist

I think the series is wonderful and beneficial for tourists to get information before visiting the city.
-Seckin Zumbul, Izmir Turkey

I am a world traveler who has read many trip guides but this one really made a difference for me. I would call it a heartfelt creation of a local guide expert instead of just a guide.
-Susy, Isla Holbox, Mexico

New to the area like me, this is a must have!
-Joe, Bloomington, USA

This is a good series that gets down to it when looking for things to do at your destination without having to read a novel for just a few ideas.
-Rachel, Monterey, USA

Good information to have to plan my trip to this destination.
-Pennie Farrell, Mexico

Aptly titled, you won't just be a tourist after reading this book. You'll be greater than a tourist!
-Alan Warner, Grand Rapids, USA

Thank you for a fantastic book.
-Don, Philadelphia, USA

Aoife Brophy

Great ideas for a port day.
-Mary Martin USA

Even though I only have three days to spend in San Miguel in an upcoming visit, I will use the author's suggestions to guide some of my time there. An easy read - with chapters named to guide me in directions I want to go.
-Robert Catapano, USA

Great insights from a local perspective! Useful information and a very good value!
-Sarah, USA

This series provides an in-depth experience through the eyes of a local. Reading these series will help you to travel the city in with confidence and it'll make your journey a unique one.
-Andrew Teoh, Ipoh, Malaysia

Tourists can get an amazing "insider scoop" about a lot of places from all over the world. While reading, you can feel how much love the writer put in it.
-Vanja Živković, Sremski Karlovci, Serbia

>TOURIST

GREATER THAN A TOURIST – GRAND CAYMAN

50 Travel Tips from a Local

Aoife Brophy

Aoife Brophy

Greater Than a Tourist- Grand Cayman Copyright © 2018 by CZYK Publishing LLC. All Rights Reserved.

All rights reserved. No part of this book may be reproduced in any form or by any electronic or mechanical means including information storage and retrieval systems, without permission in writing from the author. The only exception is by a reviewer, who may quote short excerpts in a review.

Cover Image: https://pixabay.com/en/grand-cayman-cayman-islands-1558630/

Greater Than a Tourist
Visit our website at www.GreaterThanaTourist.com

Lock Haven, PA
All rights reserved.

ISBN: 9781976947629

>TOURIST
50 TRAVEL TIPS FROM A LOCAL

Aoife Brophy

BOOK DESCRIPTION

Are you excited about planning your next trip?
Do you want to try something new?
Would you like some guidance from a local?

If you answered yes to any of these questions, then this Greater Than a Tourist book is for you.

Greater Than a Tourist- Grand Cayman by Aoife Brophy offers the inside scoop on Cayman. Most travel books tell you how to travel like a tourist. Although there is nothing wrong with that, as part of the Greater Than a Tourist series, this book will give you travel tips from someone who has lived at your next travel destination.

In these pages, you will discover advice that will help you throughout your stay. This book will not tell you exact addresses or store hours but instead will give you excitement and knowledge from a local that you may not find in other smaller print travel books.

Travel like a local. Slow down, stay in one place, and get to know the people and the culture. By the time you finish this book, you will be eager and prepared to travel to your next destination.

Aoife Brophy

>TOURIST

TABLE OF CONTENTS

BOOK DESCRIPTION
TABLE OF CONTENTS
DEDICATION
ABOUT THE AUTHOR
HOW TO USE THIS BOOK
FROM THE PUBLISHER
OUR STORY
WELCOME TO
> TOURIST
INTRODUCTION
2. ACCOMIDATIONS
3. CURRENCY AND TIPPING
4. SCUBA DIVING
5. CHILL OUT AT SEVEN MILE BEACH
6. TRY SOME JERK CHICKEN
7. VISIT EAST END
9. LITTLE CAYMAN
10. MACABUCA
11. JET SKI SAFARI
12. BRUNCH
13. ROYAL PALMS
14. MASTIC TRAIL
15. HAPPY HOUR AND NIGHTLIFE
16. WATERSPORTS
17. LOBSTER SEASON
18. CAMANA BAY

Aoife Brophy

19. WATER TAXI TO KAIBO
20. RENT MOPEDS
21. RUM POINT
22. MOSQUITOS AND SUNSCREEN
23. ENVIRONMENT
24. YOGA
25. VEGAN FOOD
26. FRESH COCONUTS
27. LIONFISH
28. TURTLE FARM
29. HORSE RIDE ON THE BEACH and in the water
30. SUPPORT THE LOCAL ARTISTS
31. Cayman Buses
32. Try a mudslide
33. groceries
34. RUM FACTORY TOUR
35. SNORKEL
36. SPOTTS BEACH
37. FLIP FLOP TREE
38. BLOW HOLES AND LOVERS WALL
39. GO TO HELL AND BACK
40. SUBMARINE TOUR
41. BIOBAY
42. CRYSTAL CAVES
43. BEST VIEW ON THE ISLAND
44. QUEEN ELIZABETH BOTANIC PARK
45. PEDRO ST JAMES CASTLE
46. WINE TASTING
47. SPA DAY

48. GOLF
49. STRING RAY CITY
50. STARFISH POINT
TOP REASONS TO BOOK THIS TRIP
> TOURIST
GREATER THAN A TOURIST
> TOURIST
GREATER THAN A TOURIST
NOTES

>TOURIST

DEDICATION

This book is dedicated to The Fresh Cash Crew.

Aoife Brophy

ABOUT THE AUTHOR

Aoife Brophy is originally from Ireland but when she was offered a job in beautiful Grand Cayman, she jumped at the chance.

Aoife learned to dive within a few months of arriving takes advantage of the weather most weekends, spending it either in the ocean, on the beach or on a boat. Despite loving Grand Cayman and considering it a second home, the Wanderlust has taken over. After two wonderful years, she is departing to travel Mexico, Central and South America.

Before she leaves, she would like to impart some insider knowledge about life in Grand Cayman. Find out where to get the best Jerk Chicken, where to go at the weekends, where to find the best diving and snorkelling and living like a local tips.

Aoife Brophy

HOW TO USE THIS BOOK

The Greater Than a Tourist book series was written by someone who has lived in an area for over three months. The goal of this book is to help travelers either dream or experience different locations by providing opinions from a local. The author has made suggestions based on their own experiences. Please do your own research before traveling to the area in case the suggested places are unavailable.

Aoife Brophy

FROM THE PUBLISHER

Traveling can be one of the most important parts of a person's life. The anticipation and memories that you have are some of the best. As a publisher of the Greater Than a Tourist book series, as well as the popular 50 Things to Know book series, we strive to help you learn about new places, spark your imagination, and inspire you. Wherever you are and whatever you do I wish you safe, fun, and inspiring travel.

Lisa Rusczyk Ed. D.
CZYK Publishing

Aoife Brophy

OUR STORY

Traveling is a passion of the "Greater than a Tourist" series creator. Lisa studied abroad in college, and for their honeymoon Lisa and her husband toured Europe. During her travels to Malta, an older man tried to give her some advice based on his own experience living on the island since he was a young boy. She was not sure if she should talk to the stranger but was interested in his advice. When traveling to some places she was wary to talk to locals because she was afraid that they weren't being genuine. Through her travels, Lisa learned how much locals had to share with tourists. Lisa created the "Greater Than a Tourist" book series to help connect people with locals. A topic that locals are very passionate about sharing.

Aoife Brophy

WELCOME TO
> TOURIST

Aoife Brophy

>TOURIST

INTRODUCTION

"Twenty years from now you will be more disappointed by the things you didn't do than by the ones you did do. So throw off the bowlines, sail away from the safe harbour. Catch the trade winds in your sails. Explore. Dream. Discover." Mark Twain

Grand Cayman is currently experiencing a huge economic boom. There has been a huge influx of expats in the last 10 years, which means that you will find a diverse range of accents on the Island. The Caymanian accent itself is quite diverse, a mix that is not quite Jamaican, not quite American and not quite English. No matter the accent, you are likely to encounter friendly people, who will go out of their way to help you. It is all part of the famous Cayman kindness.

Cars in Grand Cayman are expensive and my rust bucket broke down frequently. I never had to wait too long before someone volunteered to help me, whether I needed a jump start or a tire change. Doors are always held open for you and service comes with a smile and thank you. It was easy to make Grand Cayman my home for 2 years with such friendly locals.

Many people think of the Cayman Islands and immediately think "tax haven". It is true that there is no direct taxes but there is a story as to why. In the 1700s, several British Merchant Ships got in to distress in East End. Caymanians don't just stop to help with car trouble. They managed to rescue most of the ship's passengers, one of whom was a

Aoife Brophy

prince. The King repaid the islander's bravery by pardoning them from paying taxes. There is no hard evidence of this but for want of an alternative explanation, it has become fact.

The three islands of Grand Cayman, Little Cayman and Cayman Brac were discovered by Christopher Columbus in 1503 and were uninhabited. England took ownership in 1670 along with Jamaica in the Treaty of Madrid, who turned it into a settlement with Jamaican slaves. The main trade was turtle fishing and to this day, the Cayman Islands remains the only country in the world where it is still legal to eat turtle meat.

Perhaps that is why the Caymanians are so open to welcome expats and visitors; everyone on the island is descended from immigrants.

Due to the influences from overseas, you are likely to find a great selection of food, drink and activities compared to any other Caribbean Island. I love local food but am always happy to find food from Ireland in the supermarkets. If I really want some Irish Comfort food, I can visit the amazing Fidel Murphy's Irish Pub. You are likely to find the same no matter where in the world you are from, Grand Cayman is an international treasure in the Caribbean.

>TOURIST

1. GETTING HERE

Cayman Airways, Delta, American Airlines and Southwest Airlines fly from Atlanta, Charlotte, Havana, Kingston, Fort Lauderdale and New York. Miami is the nearest and busiest port, with flights leaving several times a day. British Airways operate a flight from London, which stops in the Bahamas for an hour either side to pick up passengers, 3 times per week.

Grand Cayman is a huge cruise ship destination of course. Carnival, Disney, Royal Caribbean and Oceania are just a few of the companies that visit Grand Cayman for the day. In busy season, there can be as many as 8 ships in, which translates to an extra 20,000 people on the small island. Traffic will be heavier than usual, as will the restaurants and bars. It is better to avoid Georgetown and these days and find a quiet stretch of beach to relax.

There are several car rental companies on island, many of which are conveniently located beside the airport. The cars are all automatic and we drive on the left side of the road. If you are staying away from Seven Mile Beach, it is absolutely necessary to rent a car as the public transport is limited. Rates are high during busy season and make sure to shop around for the best deal. With so many tourists, small road accidents are frequent. Please exercise caution and if you are not used to using roundabouts, please familiarise yourself!

2. ACCOMIDATIONS

If a nice hotel is in your budget, you are spoiled for choice. Along Seven Mile Beach you have the Ritz-Carlton, the Westin, The Kimpton, and The Marriott along with some budget options too. Expect to pay high prices during December to April. Believe it or not, the summer months are quieter and cheaper because of the heat. Many restaurants close down during the summer months altogether so please be aware of this if you plan to visit during the summer months.

Morritts in East End is a large resort that has hotel rooms and some cottages to rent if you have a family. There is a supermarket across the road as well as some restaurants and fast food options. There are also a number of smaller B&BS in Bodden Town including the Turtle Nest Inn.

For families, a condo or villa rental might be more convenient. There are several rental agencies on Island and AirBnB is a great option. Many of the properties on the island are time shares or holiday homes so they are available to rent. Apartments on Seven Mile Beach will be costly but if you are happy to rent a car and do some driving, the East End and Rum Point have some beautiful rental options to suit all budgets. Camping is illegal in the Cayman Islands except for Easter. It is an Easter tradition for families to camp out all weekend, telling stories, lighting bonfires and having barbeques. Bonfires on the beach are also illegal without a permit.

3. CURRENCY AND TIPPING

The official currency is the Cayman Islands Dollars and this is abbreviated to KYD or styled as CI$ on bills. US dollar is also accepted everywhere. Do not be afraid of being ripped off- the exchange rate is set as CI 1$ to USD$1.20.

Receipts in stores and restaurants will usually have both the Cayman Islands total and the US dollar on the bottom. ATMs will give you the choice of withdrawing either currency. Other than in smaller stores, all major credit cards are accepted.

Gratuity is included in most restaurants but be sure to check the bottom of your bill. Tipping hotel staff, resort and dive staff is customary and please note that minimum wage is just $6 CI per hour.

Aoife Brophy

4. SCUBA DIVING

Whether you are an experienced diver or you want to learn, the Cayman Islands is the place for you. There are 365 dive sites in total across the three islands. That is one for every day of the year if you want! There are several reputable dive centres on island where you can take your PADI course. It is advisable to sign up and complete your online course on the PADI website first so you can dive straight in to the practical side, pardon the pun.

Experienced divers will know that it is the luck of the dive what happens to swims by. It took me 20 dives to see a turtle but I have saw them on almost every subsequent dive. That was extremely unlucky, I was frustrated for so long especially when friends were seeing them on their first dive.

I recommend going to East End for the most unspoiled waters and the possibility of seeing one of the guys in grey suits. Reef and nurse sharks are common enough in Grand Cayman, while hammerheads are also spotted occasionally. Dolphins generally do not stay long in Cayman. A few years ago, Grand Cayman briefly hosted a frisky Dolphin called Stinky. The dolphin was known to be "over friendly" with divers but no one knows what happened to him. Hopefully he found a companion of his own species.

Sunset House is home to a Mermaid Statue and Vivo is home to a Merman Statue. Both of those locations also have coral nurseries. Eco divers have an innovative project to restore the corals around Cayman by growing new coral and replanting it. You can volunteer and have the rare opportunity to obtain the PADI qualification in Coral Conservation.

The USS Kittiwake is one of the best wreck dives in the world, because it was intentionally sunk to create an artificial reef for a dive site. Watch out for Steve, the loggerhead Turtle that lives here and a very vain Goliath Grouper that is often seen admiring himself in a mirror in one of the compartments. Tropical Storm Nate was responsible for some damage to ship in 2017 but fortunately no major damage was done.

Devil's Grotto is a shallow dive site beside Georgetown which is full of underwater caves and caverns. A huge shoal of tarpon live here, not moving or swimming. Silversides also join the tarpon during the summer months.

If you have not dived for more than two years, you will be obliged to take a refresher course for your own safety. There is a decompression chamber in the local hospital but please take the proper precautions to avoid having to use it!

Aoife Brophy

5. CHILL OUT AT SEVEN MILE BEACH

Seven Mile beach is consistently voted one of the best beaches in the world. Enjoy a beach day on a sun lounger. Bring a picnic, some snorkel gear and beach games. Don't forget the sunscreen, ice and water. Temperatures can be as high as 95 degrees in the summer.

I know several Caymanians that never go to the beach but the expats that come from colder countries definitely appreciate it. Almost everyone owns a portable barbeque which can be easily transported to the beach. We load the coolers with ice, meat, beers, ketchup and buns. Then it is a day of chilling and grilling on the beach before Monday rolls around and we are back in the office again. It's not a bad life, when every weekend is a vacation.

The beaches are cleaned regularly but watch out for sea urchins and jellyfish. The waters are usually crystal clear, so just check your area before relaxing.

6. TRY SOME JERK CHICKEN

If you like your food spicy, Grand Cayman will not disappoint.

Try Peppers Restaurant across from the Marriott for one of the best value meals in town. For under $10, you can have a full Caribbean Feast. Make sure to try some fried breadfruit, plantain and okra too, if you have never tried them. Don't forget to try Jerk Pork and Jerk Sausages too!

Try visit a local Jerk Stand if you can. When you take a drive through the island, you will smell the smoke and spice of the Jerk Stand. Fresh chicken will be barbecued before your eyes in a spicy marinade full of tasty scotch bonnet. Follow your nose and you will find men chopping and grilling chicken. It is usually served with bread and festival, which is a fried savoury donut. Street food is not as popular in Grand Cayman as it is on other Caribbean Islands so I recommend trying some Jerk.

Be sure to pick up some jerk seasoning before you leave and try to recreate your own Caribbean Chicken when you return home. Buy it in the supermarket if you can and pick up a few bottles for gifts.

Aoife Brophy

7. VISIT EAST END

East end is tranquil and traditional. The houses are old and quaint. There are restaurants in little cabanas on the side of the road where you can buy freshly caught fish for a fraction of the price and just as much taste as any of the expensive restaurants on Seven Mile Beach.

Morritt's Resort is the perfect place to spend a quiet day on a sun lounger or to do some water sports. There is a bar out on the dock that attracts some bright and colourful fish so be sure to bring your snorkel gear. If you are a diver, it is worth the early start to see the undisturbed reef.

Tukka restaurant is worth a visit especially for bird lovers. Frigate birds are the Caribbean's largest birds and you can feed them at Tukka. The birds swoop in from overhead and you hold out their dinner in a gloved hand. The food is Australian-Caribbean fusion and you can even try a kangaroo burger. Cayman is currently experiencing an invasion of green iguanas which are not native to the island. The most efficient way of getting rid of them is killing them and eating them so many restaurants on island, including Tukka are trying to incorporate them on the menus. Kangaroo burger or iguana taco, what will it be? I'm afraid I can't make any personal recommendations- I have no desire to try either!

>TOURIST

8. CAYMAN BRAC

Accommodation is limited on Cayman Brac, so make sure to book in advance particularly on long weekends. Grand Cayman residents will typically pack up their belongings, including groceries and dive gear to visit the more tranquil islands when they have the extra day off work. The Carib Sands is the main hotel on the island. There are a handful of AirBnB but make sure to book well in advance. Be advised that food will be limited on the island so if you have specific dietary requirements or require medication, come prepared.

Although there are car rental companies, the Brac is a mile wide and just 12 miles long so a bicycle is great way to get around. Like its sister, Cayman Brac is flat so take advantage of the beautiful weather and Caribbean breeze.

Cayman Brac has become a popular destination for rock climbers over the last few years. Climbing a natural limestone cliff overlooking the Caribbean Sea is the adrenaline junkie's dream. There are beginner courses too so if you have always wanted to try it, it's the perfect place.

If you are a diver, make sure to visit Captain Tibbetts wreck, a renamed sunken Russian Navy vessel.

Aoife Brophy

9. LITTLE CAYMAN

Like its name, Little Cayman is even smaller than Cayman Brac with a total population of just 150. Much of the same advice applies such as renting a bike and packing food if you have special dietary requirements. Accommodation is also limited but check out the Southern Cross Club for traditional Caribbean cottages on the beach.

You can kayak to Owen Island, a tiny uninhabited Island, relax in a hammock or do some hiking. Little Cayman is the perfect place to do nothing.

There are also several companies that run deep sea fishing charters. In deeper waters, you have the chance of seeing dolphin and swordfish as well as the chance to catch your own dinner of snapper, grouper, mahi-mahi or wahoo.

Bloody Bay wall is an unforgettable dive, consistently rated as one of the top sites in the world teaming with reef sharks, lobster, grouper and turtles.

Unfortunately, the Sister Islands are expensive to visit and because accommodation is limited, prices are high. If you are travelling in a large group, it would be best to rent a house and split the costs. It is possible to make a day trip if you would like to explore one of the islands, but possible not if you want to scuba dive to avoid decompression sickness.

10. MACABUCA

Enjoy an all you can eat sunset BBQ here on Monday nights. There are many such buffet style barbeques in Grand Cayman but Macabuca is by far the best one. Arrive early to dive or snorkel Turtle Reef, then fill you bellies with delicious Caribbean food (and maybe a mudslide or 5).

This was one of the first places I visited when I arrived on island. I remember being on Skype with my family and making them very jealous of the view in the background. It is a Tiki style bar with beautiful food, although it suffers from flooding in stormy weather. Check their website for a live webcam if you can't wait to see the view in person. For a more upmarket dinner, try the Cracked Conch restaurant upstairs. This offers beautiful views and a full service cocktail bar.

This is also a great night dive sight. It is very easy to navigate but if you aren't confident, the dive company Sundivers, run regular guided night dives.

Aoife Brophy

11. JET SKI SAFARI

Most hotels offer jet ski rental but you are confined a certain space marked by buoys. Hit the open water on a Jet Ski Safari to Stingray City, Starfish Point and lunch at the beautiful beach bar and restaurant Kaibo. You can also snorkel in the middle of the sea and observe Cayman's pristine reefs and fish. I love this tour and think that it is by far the best way to explore. If you have never been on a Jet-Ski before, you will be given a full briefing and test-ride first.

It is not a legal requirement to wear a life jacket but the company may insist and rightly so. There is a free shuttle service from the Hard Rock Cafe provided by the company, Fat Fish Adventures.

12. BRUNCH

If you thought that brunch was Eggs Benedict think again. The Cayman Brunch is an all afternoon Sunday affair. Beginning at 12pm with a glass of Prosecco (the glass is bottomless, if you don't get distracted by the food). There is a breakfast, seafood, cheese, soup, bread and main course counter. A selection of desserts is also included if you still have room. I thought a brunch was something like a large breakfast or small lunch but the Cayman brunch is a new level of feasting.

If you are a picky eater, there will be something for you and if you are a foodie, you will be in heaven. Try the Kimpton, The Marriot and the Ritz-Carlton. Arrive hungry and not with a hangover.

If there is a large party, be sure to book your table in advance, particularly when there is a public holiday the following day. That is when we locals are most likely to indulge in a brunch-when we have an extra day off after to recover!

13. ROYAL PALMS

After brunch, if you survive the bottomless Prosecco, go to Royal Palms. When the rest of Seven Mile was being born, Royal Palms was the only place to be. Literally. It was one of the only bars on Seven Mile Beach for several years but it is still a local favourite.

Rent a cabana or lie on a sun lounger, it is actually a good idea to wear a swimsuit under your brunch clothes. Otherwise, make sure to pack one along with a towel and sunscreen. Carry on drinking with the friendly locals and expats until sunset and be grateful you are on vacation and don't have to work tomorrow.

Royal Palms also opens all week long and serves food. There is a reasonably priced water sports rental company, if you are feeling adventurous. They have pool parties on Wednesday nights complete with a selection of pool float.

14. MASTIC TRAIL

This trail is a 5 mile round walk and can be completed in under 2 hours. The area is unspoiled and protected by government. It is the perfect chance to spot a rare Cayman Parrot who are bright green with a red face. You are more likely to hear one than see one because they camouflage well in the trees and emit a high pitched screech.

There are some small snakes plenty of iguanas. None of the animals in Grand Cayman are dangerous in any way unless cornered. Watch out for agoutis, a rodent like creature I had never heard of before moving here. They are like a rabbit or large guinea pig and come from Central America. They are not typically on menus here but a Caymanian lady that I work with told me she used to eat them as a child.

The Mastic Tree was traditionally used in shipbuilding but has declined significantly in population due to deforestation. In summer, watch out for mango trees, almond trees and papaya trees. The fresh mangos in the summer are incredible.

Aoife Brophy

15. HAPPY HOUR AND NIGHTLIFE

Most of the bars offer happy hour prices on all drinks including cocktails from 5pm to 7pm. This is usually when bars are busiest especially on Friday nights after work. Remember that everywhere closes at 12pm on a Saturday, so if you want a late night out, Friday is your best option.

Some of the best places for Happy Hour include Rackham's, Hemingway's, Bar Crudo and Sunset House.

If you feel like carrying in the night, head to Borolo's, Calicos Jacks or Whiskey Mist. Lilies is the Islands only nightclub and opens until 4am in Fridays. Calicos is the best place to go on Saturday nights.

16. WATERSPORTS

Unfortunately, the currents are rarely strong enough for surfing. Wind and Kite Surfing are popular but expensive. There are several rental companies in West Bay, as well as private lessons if you are just beginning.

For the less adventurous water lovers, there is stand up paddle boarding, kayaking and sailing, all available from most hotels. Deep sea fishing charters are available from local fisherman.

17. LOBSTER SEASON

The Caribbean Lobster are not as attractive as their red Maine cousins, but they are delicious! Please note that poaching is illegal and lobster season runs from December 1st until February 28th. If you are lucky enough to be here for the Christmas period you will definitely see it on menus in some restaurant, if you are not feeling brave enough to catch your own. If you are an experienced lobster hunter, then please be advised that there is a limit of 3 per person and the Department of the Environment imposes hefty fines on those poaching. Fat Fish Adventures offer a Lobster catching and cooking tour during the season.

Aoife Brophy

18. CAMANA BAY

Cayman's newest town has been developing for the last few years. Several shops, restaurants and bars have opened in this hub of activity.

There are always free activities such as outdoor movies happening in Camana Bay so be sure to check the website when you arrive to see what is happening. There is playground and water fountains for the kids to play.

Take a stroll around the shops, have a coffee and enjoy a waterside meal in Mizu, Brooklyn or Karoo. I also recommend trying an Italian Gelato from Gelato and Co. There is an artificial island where you can read a book in a hammock. The farmer and artisan market takes place there every Wednesday.

If you are unlucky with some bad weather, there is a movie theatre which includes a VIP section that serves pizza and snacks while you recline in a comfy seat.

Bon Vivant also offers various cookery classes; from sushi making to fish to Asian and Italian. I also recommend taking the food tour, which is inspired by farm to table cuisine. On Wednesday nights, the tour departs and takes you a selection of the restaurants and bars to sample a few dishes and drinks from each one. Perfect if you can't decide what to eat.

>TOURIST

19. WATER TAXI TO KAIBO

While you're in Camana Bay, take a water Taxi out to the beautiful restaurant Upstairs at Kaibo. Try one of their cocktails and feel like you have stepped back to the 1920s, with the great Gatsby decor in the Rare Rum Bar. Here you will find Cayman's best selection of aged rums and they offer a tasting if you are a rum connoisseur.

If you want, you can have a dinner cooked by a Michelin Star Chef and the 8 course tasting menu is great value for the quality of food you receive.

It is certainly one of Grand Cayman's best kept secrets and I'm certain they don't put it in the tour guides. In fact, it is highly in demand by residents so do remember to book in advance to avoid disappointment especially on Friday and Saturday nights.

20. RENT MOPEDS

If you are short on time and perhaps just off the cruise ship for the day, rent a moped to see the off the beaten bath. It is the best way to escape the tourist centred shops and see the real Grand Cayman with its beautiful beaches, limestone formations and palm trees.

Moped rental is $50 US for the day and you can explore the island at your leisure. Grab a map and remember the island is small, so you can't get lost for long.

21. RUM POINT

Rum point on Saturdays and Sundays is usually teeming with boats of residents and tourists.

Witness the locals let their hair down on dancing on their boats and swimming around. Small boats to super yachts dock to take advantage of the blue waters and sunshine. Try a mudslide at the bar and catch a hammock or better yet bring your own. Sit back, relax and watch the windsurfers.

There is also a nice restaurant to have dinner, a jerk stand, cabanas and plenty of photo opportunities.

22. MOSQUITOS AND SUNSCREEN

Fortunately, the mosquitos in Grand Cayman are not disease carrying. However they are still a nuisance especially around dawn and dusk. There is a natural repellent called Medela which is sold everywhere. It smells of lemongrass, a much better scent than the chemical ones. It comes in a green bottle.

Grand Caymans close location to the Equator makes it a beautiful tropical destination but it also means that the UV rays are stronger. Make sure to wear sunscreen and reapply every few hours. Even if the day is cloudy, please be careful especially if you are prone to burning. Make sure to allow your sunscreen to dry before entering the water for at least 20 minutes.

Wear a hat, sunglasses and bring rash vests for the kids.

Aoife Brophy

23. ENVIRONMENT

Remember to leave no trace in the Cayman Islands. That means to bring rubbish with you when you're leaving the beach and dispose of it correctly. Please avoid using straws where possible or take up the offer of using a paper straw. One local company called Peripheral, has recently started to sell glass straws. Make sure to let your sunscreen dry in before entering the ocean. Try to recycle if you are in your own accommodation. Use reusable bags where possible and bring a water bottle to refill. The supermarkets have a wide range of ecofriendly products including personal hygiene products and sunscreen.

24. YOGA

If you are a Yogi, there is an amazing studio called Bliss, where you can purchase guest passes for a single class or for the week. If you have never tried yoga, now is your chance. Let the teachers know that it is your first class and they will be happy to give you some extra guidance. Take time out to mediate and stretch. Choose from Hot, Power, Flow and Yin. They also run regular workshops, meditation days and have a beautiful store to purchase books and clothing.

As well as this, there are several beach sessions run by some of the hotels and by private teachers. The idea of beach yoga seems appealing, but it is actually a lot more difficult as the sand isn't solid.

If you would like to combine your love of the water and your love of yoga, try a paddle-yoga session, which is run by several companies on island including one I recommend called Vitamin Sea.

25. VEGAN FOOD

Cayman is home to a wonderful Vegan Restaurant called Bread and Chocolate. If the fresh fish and jerk chicken does not appeal, you will not be disappointed with the food here. Along with the tastiest soups and healthiest salads, there are also plant based treats such as vegan pizza, burgers and sweet dairy free desserts. Recently they have opened up for an evening restaurant service, serving meals such as Pulled Porkless Sliders, Vegan Pizza, Three Tacos and Vegan Cheesecake. The owners are friendly and happy to help with your choices. If you are passing by there and need a sugar hit, I recommend the chocolate chip cookies; my usual Friday treat.

26. FRESH COCONUTS

Coconut Water is the elixir of life. Hangover? Coconut water. Dehydrated? Coconut Water. Sick tummy/cold coming on? Coconut water. Full of potassium and electrolytes, this healthy drink will revitalise and refresh.

There are several vendors in Georgetown and along Seven Mile that will chop a fresh coconut with a machete to cure whatever ails you. Of course you don't have to be sick to enjoy one! I'm a little obsessed.

27. LIONFISH

Lionfish is an invasive species which is a huge threat to the resident aquatic species. The best solution is to eat it, as it is a tasty and meaty fish.

You do need a licence to hunt lionfish as their sting is venomous. Please do not approach them if you are diving. I have a licence but have never managed to successfully kill one. I can confirm that they are tasty and extremely difficult to fillet.

Head to Vivo in West Bay to try Lionfish Ceviche and Tacos. The Westin Hotel also sponsors Lionfish culls the first Sunday of every month and serves the fresh catch in the restaurant.

One local also had the idea of making the spines into jewellery. The pieces are available from Vivo and Pure Art. They are really beautiful and make an original souvenir or gift.

Aoife Brophy

28. TURTLE FARM

The Cayman Islands is the only place in the world it is legal to eat Turtle meat. Most people say it tastes like beef. Visit the Turtle farm in West Bay to hold a baby turtle, try Cayman Turtle Stew and enjoy the small water park.

There is a conservation program but the turtles there are raised for meat. Some of the turtles are bred in captivity and released in the wild. Turtle populations fell rapidly in the 1800s but with the turtle centres conservation problem, this is starting to improve. Unfortunately, Hurricane Ivan in 2004 also had a negative impact on the turtle population but they are starting to increase once again.

29. HORSE RIDE ON THE BEACH AND IN THE WATER

Caymans Horses like to swim! Take a sunset horse ride along the beach and wear clothes that you don't mind getting wet. This tour lasts about an hour and departs from Breakers Beach in West Bay. This part of the island is home to dense Mangroves, which are trees that grow in water. These trees are an essential part of the ecosystem and protect Grand Cayman from storm surges as well as being home to lots of wildlife.

The sunset horse ride on the beach and a dinner at the beautiful Italian restaurant, Pappagallo would be the perfect romantic evening, just remember to bring a change of clothes!

Aoife Brophy

30. SUPPORT THE LOCAL ARTISTS

Despite being a small island, Grand Cayman is home to a great deal of talented artists and writers. Take a browse in the National Gallery, which is located in the middle of Georgetown has various exhibits and events year round.

Pure Art on South Church Street is worth a visit. It hosts paintings from several local artists, glassware, sculpture, handmade candles, jewellery and other souvenirs. It is worth the short drive out of town to get lost for a few hours in this tiny gallery set in an old style Caymanian cottage. The owners are really friendly and helpful. Almost every gift I have bought on island, I have bought here.

Three Girls and a Kiln are a local pottery business that make beautiful handmade pieces.

Cathy Church is an award winning photographer based in sunset house. If you are a budding photographer, lessons in photography and underwater photography are available.

Books and Books in Camana Bay has a section dedicated to Caymanian authors if you are in need of a vacation read.

>TOURIST

31. CAYMAN BUSES

Cayman does not have sufficient population to sustain an effective public transport system. Nonetheless, you will be able to get around on the local minibuses if you are not in a hurry. This is a great way to talk to locals who are really friendly.

Fairs are flat at $2 KYD or $2:50 USD whether you are travelling a short distance or all the way to East End.

Shout "Want stop" when you want to stop. (Really!)

There are taxi companies on island which look exactly like the public buses. They are quite expensive and not very reliable.

32. TRY A MUDSLIDE

Do not leave Cayman without trying a mudslide.

Many establishments claim to have the best one but Rum Point Club claims to have invented it in the 1970s when a customer asked for a White Russian but they had no milk. The barman improvised with Vodka, Kahlua, Baileys, Ice-cream with an extra shot of Kailua down the straw, whipped cream and cherry on top. Make sure to have a designated driver.

This drink is part drink and part dessert and you can get a non-alcoholic version for the kids.

33. GROCERIES

If you are renting an apartment, shopping at grocery stores and doing your own cooking can save a lot of money. Kirks and Fosters are the two main supermarkets and I recommend checking both as they both stock different brands. They both have delis and hot food bars which are good value and delicious. Kirks is slightly higher end and more expensive.

You should be able to find everything that you need and more. With such a diverse expat community there are British, Irish, South African and Jamaican sections to name just a few as well as section for locally grown vegetables. Farming in Grand Cayman is limited to although there is some local beef, most items are imported either from the United States or Jamaica.

Please be advised that all of the supermarkets close on Sundays, so make sure to stock up on Saturday. Gas Stations remain open and stock essentials such as bread and milk. Supermarkets do not sell alcohol so if you are planning on a boozy Sunday, stock up in the liquor store in advance.

Aoife Brophy

34. RUM FACTORY TOUR

The distillery offers a great tasting tour with several generous samples. (Don't be afraid to ask for seconds!) Try the famous Caribbean Rum Cake, a yellow cake fed with rum. The rum is really reasonably priced here. If you are a cruise ship passenger or visitor, you can avail of duty free prices. The bottles will be available for pick up at the airport or the cruise ship port for collection.

35. SNORKEL

Bring your own gear or rent from one of the many companies on Island. Float on the surface on check out the marine life below. Eden Rock and Devil's Grotto are great locations in Georgetown. It is shallow and close to shore but you will see an abundance of fish and maybe a turtle if you are lucky!

In Georgetown, there is also the Cali shipwreck just 40 yards from shore. You can even see the shadow from land, it is just a few feet under the surface.

There are also several companies offering snorkel trips further out to the reefs. With so much fantastic snorkelling available from the shore, it is not really necessary, unless you are already taking a boat trip or Jet Ski safari.

36. SPOTTS BEACH

This is a great place to see turtles in the wild. The turtles are attracted to this area because of there is an abundance of sea grass for them to feed on. All of the Turtles in Cayman are tagged to keep an eye on population and poaching. During turtle mating season, the turtles come ashore to lay their eggs so please be careful not to disturb any nests.

You can snorkel with Turtles at chest or even waist depth, so if you are not confident in water but want to see a turtle in the wild go to Spott's Beach. Be aware that the sea here has strong currents, so please remember to swim within your abilities. That said, it is the perfect location for snorkelling. The waters are crystal clear and there are very few boats. Look for heavy concentrations of snorkelers as that is where you will find the Turtles. There is a boardwalk too where you can usually spot the Turtles shadows before getting in the Water. I have also seen plenty of Stingrays here along with every fish imaginable.

There aren't any shops nearby so be sure to pack a picnic and a cooler full of ice and water. There are cabanas and benches so it is the perfect place to have a quiet beach day, with plenty of shade if it gets too hot.

Aoife Brophy

37. FLIP FLOP TREE

A local couple started this tree to raise awareness about pollution after witnessing all of the plastic that washes up on Grand Cayman. The couple were shocked that they could fill a bag of rubbish each time they visited the beach and decided to do something to highlight the issue. It is an unfortunate fact that if you walk the beaches away from Seven Mile, every kind of plastic shoes up. Toothbrushes, toys, bottles, and for some reason, many shoes. The Island was submerged by Hurricane Ivan in 2004 and it is thought that debris is still washing up many years later.

The idea grew and soon people were travelling from all over the island to nail their broken flip flops to the tree. Campaigns like this have done there party in ensuring that Grand Cayman is gradually becoming more environmentally friendly.

38. BLOW HOLES AND LOVERS WALL

The Blow Holes are a limestone formation where the water rushed through and then shoots upwards like a whale's blow hole. Hurricane Ivan destroyed some of the formations but most of it still remains. There is a beautiful coastal drive out to East and it is worth making a stop off here.

Lovers Wall is located just beside. No one really knows why it is called that other that it being a romantic photo opportunity for you and the other half.

39. GO TO HELL AND BACK

Hell is the name of a little area in West Bay that is home to a limestone formation that literally looks like Hell. Get a picture with the devil and grab a postcard to verify your trip to hell and back in the small post office and gift shop, "The Devil's Hangout"

The main attraction of Hell is probably the store's owner, Ivan, who sports a red cape, horns and a goatee to greet visitors. He says that the area was originally called Paradise but his business was failing so he re-branded in the opposite direction.

Aoife Brophy

40. SUBMARINE TOUR

Cayman is a diver's paradise, but if diving is not for you, there is another way to venture underwater without even getting wet. The Atlantis Submarine Tour takes you to see the underwater mermaid statue and along Eden Rock.

The Mermaid Statue is a 9 foot 600 pound statue at Sunset House. She is officially named Amphitrite, Siren of Sunset Reef. In mythology, Amphitrite was the queen of the seas, married to Poseidon, lord of the oceans and the statue was installed there in 2000. The submarine tour also takes you on a tour of the reef. Make sure to keep your eyes on the window or you might miss something!

Sunset House is a popular dive because of the Statue. I recommend bringing your underwater camera for a rare photo opportunity.

\> TOURIST

41. BIOBAY

Away from the bright lights of Seven mile, close to Starfish point, a small bay lights up at night with bioluminescent plankton. You can choose to Paddle-Board or Kayak. It is better to go when it is dark as possible so that it is more visible.

Bioluminescence is a natural phenomenon where a living organism produces light, such as fireflies. While bioluminescence is common in the seas and oceans, it is rare to find it in such high concentrations where it is clearly visible to the naked eye and so close to shore. They react to touch, so when you but in your oar, the bioluminescence sparkle around you.

This tour departs from Rum Point. If you do not have a rental car, the company runs shuttle buses from Seven Mile to the location. It is best to bring a change of clothes especially if you are an inexperienced paddle boarder!

42. CRYSTAL CAVES

These caves have only been open to the public in recent years and in fact they were only discovered in the 1990s. For most of the island's history, no humans had entered apart from maybe some Pirates to hide their treasure. The project of making the caves fit for tourists took over 20 years but now you can take a guided tour through the forest and down through the caverns below ground. If you have a phobia of bats, it is probably best avoided but they are usually asleep during the day tours and are harmless.

The tour takes around an hour and a half but is located near rum point. There are shuttle services if you don't have a car.

43. BEST VIEW ON THE ISLAND

Grand Cayman is famously flat. If you want the best view of the island, it is on a helicopter. Jerome, your pilot will bring you on a tour of Seven Mile and out towards North Side. It is a really fun way of taking in the view of the white beaches and clear water. It was my first time in a helicopter so I really loved it. Jerome, the pilot is very professional and makes you feel safe.

>TOURIST

44. QUEEN ELIZABETH BOTANIC PARK

This beautiful Park is located a 40 minute drive from Georgetown. It is worth the trip to walk around the beautiful gardens and to see some wildlife.

You can learn about the Blue Iguana breeding program from the experts. Blue Iguanas are the only native species on the island are endangered. Green Iguanas are invasive to the island and are currently threatening the Native Blue Iguana. As I mentioned above, the government is trying to solve this problem by introducing them to the local cuisine.

The flowers and gardens are spectacular. There is a lake and woodland trail so it is the perfect place to have a picnic. Make sure to pack something as there is no restaurant on site or anywhere close by.

Aoife Brophy

45. PEDRO ST JAMES CASTLE

This building is the oldest on island and was owned by one of the first plantation settlers, William Eden. It is located in Bodden Town, the original Capital of Grand Cayman. The house was used as the Cayman Islands first House of Parliament in 1831. The house fell into disrepair for many years and was severely damaged by various storms until a huge renovation project was undertaken in 1996.

There is a theatre where you can watch an informative video about Cayman's history and it is a popular destination for weddings and other social events. The views are beautiful and there is a gift shop and small café.

46. WINE TASTING

The Tasting Rooms is a hidden gem if you are a wine lover, foodie and want an extravagant treat. The decor is rustic and has an old fashioned tavern feel. The walls are lined bottles of wine and books. The owner Mario, is hospitable and knowledgeable. There is an option to do wine tastings and pairings with food. I recommend eating here as the food is really fantastic.

Some of the wines are affordable and there are discounts for purchasing several bottles. The company also offers a villa stocking service, so that if you get off your flight and just want to kick back with a glass of wine to start your vacation, there will be a bottle waiting for you

Aoife Brophy

47. SPA DAY

There are numerous day spas on the island to suit every budget. If you are feeling extravagant, the Westin offers a Massage on the Beach in the privacy of a Cabana. I was treated to a Spa Day at the Ritz Carlton for my birthday and I recommend taking your time to enjoy all of the facilities.

Many of the day spas have special offers and discounts during the week. It is competitive and all of them offer a high quality Service. I recommend Bodyworks which Reiki and Aromatherapy massage.

There are also several mobile masseuse services on island if you don't want to leave your room such as Perfectly Pampered.

The Marriott and the Ritz-Carlton also offer a beautiful afternoon tea if you are searching for the ultimate girls day out.

48. GOLF

Cayman boasts two spectacular Golf Courses in both the Ritz-Carlton and North Sound Golf Club.

North Sound Golf Club offers 18 holes for $130 but why not take advantage of the $55 twilight rate? After 3pm is the best time to Golf in the Caribbean, when the sun is starting to set and the heat is fading. There is also a driving range and if you really want to work on your game, you can get a few lessons from a PGA professional.

The Ritz is pricier but a better course. Expect to pay $200USD for 9 holes.

Aoife Brophy

49. STRING RAY CITY

Have you ever fed a stingray? Now is your chance. In the middle of the islands, there is a sandbar. This means that in the middle of the ocean, the sea floor rises up so that you can stand up to your waist on a calm day. This has attracted tourists for a few years as it is home to several friendly stingrays. They are tame and used to people but come with some squid or they will be disappointed!

You can take a boat tour here or stop of on the Jet-Ski Safari. I recommend coming with an experienced local, as there is a special technique to catching a stingray. Feeding one is fun, but be quick! They don't have teeth but their kiss will give you a bruise and 7 years good luck.

The breed that occupy the water here are Southern Stingrays and they are generally safe to swim with. That said, exercise caution not to step on any or corner them. It is thought that they were attracted to the area by fishermen who would throw away their bait after a day's work as they were returning back to the docks in West Bay.

>TOURIST

50. STARFISH POINT

The next stop on the boat tour is usually Starfish point, where you will usually find dozens of starfish washed up in the shallow water. Please remember that they are living creatures and that if they are taken out of the water, they die. You can pick them up and take a picture, but please make sure that they remain submerged in the water. This beach is a great place to relax for a few hours.

Aoife Brophy

TOP REASONS TO BOOK THIS TRIP

It is the perfect mix of old and new: Enjoy the modern development of seven mile and the more traditional East End

It has one of the best beaches in the world: do you need another reason?

The people are friendly: Cayman is one of the safest places that I have ever been and you can wander the off the beaten path without any fear.

The scuba diving is spectacular: Grand Cayman has some of the clearest, warmest waters in the world.

Aoife Brophy

> TOURIST
GREATER THAN A TOURIST

Visit GreaterThanATourist.com:
http://GreaterThanATourist.com

Sign up for the Greater Than a Tourist Newsletter:
http://eepurl.com/cxspyf

Follow us on Facebook:
https://www.facebook.com/GreaterThanATourist

Follow us on Pinterest:
http://pinterest.com/GreaterThanATourist

Follow us on Instagram:
http://Instagram.com/GreaterThanATourist

Aoife Brophy

> TOURIST
GREATER THAN A TOURIST

Please leave your honest review of this book on Amazon and Goodreads. Thank you. We appreciate your positive and constructive feedback. Thank you.

Aoife Brophy

NOTES

Made in the USA
Lexington, KY
11 September 2019